AN ADULT COLORING BOOK

Live Loved

Craft God's Word Into Your Heart

Through Creative Expression

BETHANY HOUSE
a division of Baker Publishing Group
Minneapolis, Minnesota

LIVE LOVED

An Adult Coloring Book by Margaret Feinberg

Craft God's Word Into Your Heart
Through Creative Expression

Copyright © 2015 by Margaret Feinberg (www.margaretfeinberg.com)

Published by Bethany House Publishers
11400 Hampshire Avenue South
Bloomington, Minnesota 55438
www.bethanyhouse.com

Bethany House Publishers is a division of
Baker Publishing Group, Grand Rapids, Michigan

Printed in the United States of America

ISBN 978-0-7642-1862-0

Scripture quotations identified as NIV are from the Holy Bible, New International Version®. NIV®. Copyright © 1973, 1978, 1984, 2011 by Biblica, Inc.™ Used by permission of Zondervan. All rights reserved worldwide. www.zondervan.com

Scripture quotations identified as NLT are from the *Holy Bible*, New Living Translation, copyright © 1996, 2004, 2007 by Tyndale House Foundation. Used by permission of Tyndale House Publishers, Inc., Carol Stream, Illinois 60188. All rights reserved.

Scripture quotations identified as TLB are from *The Living Bible*, copyright © 1971. Used by permission of Tyndale House Publishers, Inc., Wheaton, Illinois 60189. All rights reserved.

Scripture quotations identified as MESSAGE are from *The Message* by Eugene H. Peterson, copyright © 1993, 1994, 1995, 2000, 2001, 2002. Used by permission of NavPress Publishing Group. All rights reserved.

Scripture quotations identified as NASB are from the New American Standard Bible®, copyright © 1960, 1962, 1963, 1968, 1971, 1972, 1973, 1975, 1977, 1995 by The Lockman Foundation. Used by permission.

Scripture quotations identified as ESV are from The Holy Bible, English Standard Version® (ESV®), copyright © 2001 by Crossway, a publishing ministry of Good News Publishers. Used by permission. All rights reserved. ESV Text Edition: 2007

Scripture quotations identified as NKJV are from the New King James Version. Copyright © 1982 by Thomas Nelson, Inc. Used by permission. All rights reserved.

Scripture quotations identified as EXB are from The Expanded Bible. Copyright © 2011 by Thomas Nelson. Used by permission. All rights reserved.

Scripture quotations identified as HCSB are from the Holman Christian Standard Bible, copyright 1999, 2000, 2002, 2003 by Holman Bible Publishers. Used by permission.

Scripture quotations identified as NRSV are from the New Revised Standard Version of the Bible, copyright © 1989, by the Division of Christian Education of the National Council of the Churches of Christ in the United States of America. Used by permission. All rights reserved.

16 17 18 19 20 21 22   12 11 10 9 8 7 6

Meet Margaret

A self-described "hot mess," Margaret Feinberg is a popular Bible teacher and speaker at churches and leading conferences such as Catalyst, Thrive, and Women of Joy. Her books, including *The Organic God*, *The Sacred Echo*, *Scouting the Divine*, *Wonderstruck*, and *Fight Back With Joy* and their corresponding Bible studies, have sold nearly one million copies and received critical acclaim and extensive national media coverage from CNN, the Associated Press, *USA Today*, the *Los Angeles Times*, *The Washington Post*, and more.

She was recently named one of 50 women most shaping culture and the church today by *Christianity Today*, one of the 30 voices who will help lead the church in the next decade by *Charisma Magazine,* and one of the 40 who will shape Christian publishing by *Christian Retailing* magazine. Margaret and her husband, Leif, have an adorable superpup named Hershey. She believes some of the best days are spent in jammies, laughing, and being silly.

Let's be friends

🌐 margaretfeinberg.com

f Margaret Feinberg

🐦 @mafeinberg

📷 @mafeinberg

✉ hello@margaretfeinberg.com

Learning to live loved

One evening, I grabbed a bite to eat with my friend Naomi. She shared the details of a complicated conflict between her and a coworker. The key to resolving the disagreement was recognizing that she was operating out of an area of insecurity that had haunted her since childhood. With this realization, she renewed her efforts to work hard and well with the coworker. The irritant in the relationship disappeared.

"That's one of those cases of learning to live loved," she said.

"What do you mean?" I asked.

"Living as if we're loved by God instead of responding out of the usual petty jealousies, insecurities, fears, or annoyances that try to get the best of us."

"Live loved." The syllables somersaulted off my lips. "I like that."

The phrase followed me home. The words didn't just capture the heart of the greatest commandments—to love God and others—but struck me as crucial, even foundational, for abounding in joy.

Apart from love, our potential for experiencing joy remains flat like a lifeless balloon. Love exhales the fullness of joy.

As God's love breathes in and through us, the balloons of joy begin to expand in our lives. Our spirits experience levity. We find ourselves surrounded by gladness and cheer and delight. Soon we cannot help but laugh and play and rejoice in gratitude at being God's children.

Love exhales the fullness of joy.

It all begins with love.

How would my attitude, actions, and reactions change if I lived in the unconditional, immeasurable love of God? How would my relationships with others be impacted if I learned to allow God's love to flow in and through me? Would my capacity for joy expand if I learned to live loved?

If I want to live loved, where should I begin?

I compiled a list of Scriptures that reveal God's love.

As I jotted down a few notes, I began to wonder, *How have I lived my whole life as a Christian and never sought God's love to infuse me like this? Shouldn't this be the foundation of my life?*

God, fill me with your love anew, I prayed. *I want to live loved.*

I began spending 5 to 10 minutes each day marinating in the truth of God's love found in Scripture. I used the time to read, reflect, and even memorize passages that reveal God's boundless love and to ask God for His love to overflow in my life.

I still remember that first morning. I set a timer suspecting ten minutes might feel long, but the time passed all too soon. Reading through the promises of God's steadfast, enduring, and unfailing love, my eyes became damp. I took a slow, deep breath and exhaled in an effort to hold back the tiny water droplets. The response welled up like a wave and broke over my soul.

God, fill me with your love anew. I want to live loved.

These tears weren't stained by sadness; they were marked by joy.

When I regained my composure, I realized the Scriptures exposed just how much I question and doubt God's love. On far too many days, God's love doesn't feel tangible or real. Though I often proclaim God's love to others, such divine affection often feels like it's for someone else, not me. Yet the passages reveal God's love is closer, more faithful, more present, than I realize in my day-to-day life.

Each of us has quiet phrases that accompany us through life. Though we seldom give voice to them, some of the most common passengers include:

Am I really loved?
Am I loveable?
Do I really belong?
Does it make a difference that I exist?
Does what I do matter?

Outside of extraordinary circumstances or the safety of intimate friendship, these questions are almost never spoken aloud, yet they lurk in the shadows of our actions and responses to others. Most of us recognize these questions in others long before we identify them in ourselves.

One of my closest friends has wrestled with knowing that she's loved since I've known her. Over the course of our fifteen-year friendship, I've expressed how much I adore and appreciate her countless times. My efforts to fill her with love feel like trying to fill a bottomless well one tablespoon at a time.

Somewhere in the recesses of her heart, she keeps asking "Am I loved?" Because of our long-time relationship, I even know some of the reasons why. But as loud and as often as I affirm, "You're loved more than you can possibly imagine!", the words seem to bounce off her heart. Though I continue to affirm her, I know that the only one who can satisfy her is God.

Yet how often am I the one with the aching questions?

I'm all too aware of my faults and failures, my shortcoming and missteps. I'd never ask you, "Am I loveable?", but I'll spend more time than you'll ever know orchestrating an adorable outfit, winsome responses, and affable time together. If afterward, you offer some form of affirmation or accolade, I'll flick your words away. "It's nothing at all." Yet I wish you'd say more. Maybe then your words might dull the ache that accompanies the doubts I have of being lovable.

The tears running down my face signaled that I'd been turning to sources other than God to receive love and answer my deepest heart questions.

God alone can provide the responses to the unspoken questions we wake up with each day. He longs to speak into our deepest doubts, our most mangled fears. Through the pages of Scripture, I began to see the abundant love of God isn't just for everyone else, but for you and me:

- "I have loved you with an everlasting love; I have drawn you with unfailing kindness" (Jeremiah 31:3 NIV).
- "The mountains may move and the hills disappear, but even then my faithful love for you will remain" (Isaiah 54:10 NLT).
- "I paid a huge price for you. . . . *That's* how much you mean to me! *That's* how much I love you! I'd sell off the whole world to get you back, trade the creation just for you" (Isaiah 43:4 MESSAGE).
- "The Lord your God is with you; the mighty One will save you. He will rejoice over you. You will rest in his love; he will sing and be joyful about you" (Zephaniah 3:17 EXB).

Through these verses and others, the truth that we are loved and loveable to God can pour through us and cleanse us. Though we may struggle to see ourselves as loved or lovely, the lens of Scripture can correct our vision, allowing us to see what God sees.

That's why I've created *Live Loved: An Adult Coloring Book*. Within these pages, you'll find hand-selected Scriptures that speak to God's love for you and how His love is meant to flow through you to others.

We live in a world where we're constantly pressed by demands on every side—from our work, our home, our families. While many of these demands are good, if they stack too high, they can squeeze the life and creativity out of us. We can become too busy to slow down, recalibrate, and pursue creative outlets.

Marinate in the truth of God's fierce love for you.

Live Loved: An Adult Coloring Book provides an opportunity for you to

- Spend time praying and reflecting to grow in your relationship with God
- Commit Bible passages to memory to deepen your faith
- Marinate in the truth of God's fierce love for you and experience transformation
- Express your love for God and the Bible through creativity
- Strengthen relationships as you invite others to create alongside you
- Share your artistry with others as you show off your work

My hope and prayer is that through the upcoming pages, you'll unleash the creative talents God has given you. Color and sketch, whisper the words aloud, commit them to memory, and learn how to live loved in a tangible way.

Blessings,

Margaret

How to use this book

Playing with color and paint is good for grown-ups, too. Here are some ideas to get the best use of this adult coloring book:

- Gather your favorite coloring supplies—colored pencils, crayons, markers, or paint.
- Read through the verse. Meander. Pause. Reflect.
- Circle or underline particularly meaningful phrases. Which ones are new to you?
- Keep a Bible nearby to look up the context for any passages that are particularly intriguing to you.
- Turn to a biblical dictionary or commentary for extra understanding.
- Commit the verse to memory as you color. Remember: No need to stay in the lines. Be as creative as you'd like.
- Use the journaling page adjacent to the coloring page to write down any thoughts, doodles, reflections, or prayers.
- Finish your time with prayer: *Lord, how do you want me to live today in light of your love?*
- Share what you create! Snap a photo and share on social media using #liveloved.

pray & reflect

"See what kind of love the Father has given to us
that we should be called children of God; and so we are."
—1 John 3:1 ESV

See what
kind of love
the Father
has given to us that
we should be called
children of God
and so we are.

1 JOHN 3:1

pray & reflect

"As the Father has loved me, so I have loved you.
Now remain in my love."
—John 15:9 NIV

As the Father has loved me, so I have loved you. Now remain in my love.

JOHN 15:9

pray & reflect

"I have loved you with an everlasting love;
I have drawn you with unfailing kindness."
—Jeremiah 31:3 NIV

I have
loved you with
an everlasting love;
I have drawn you with
unfailing kindness.

JEREMIAH 31:3

pray & reflect

"I paid a huge price for you. . . . *That's* how much you mean to me!
That's how much I love you!"
—Isaiah 43:4 MESSAGE

I paid a huge price for you...
That's how much you mean to me!
That's how much I love you!

ISAIAH 43:4

pray & reflect

"But God demonstrates His own love toward us,
in that while we were still sinners, Christ died for us."
—Romans 5:8 NKJV

But God demonstrates his own love toward us, in that while we were still sinners, Christ died for us.

ROMANS 5:8

pray & reflect

"Because of the Lord's great love we are not consumed,
for his compassions never fail."
—Lamentations 3:22 NIV

Because of the Lord's great love we are not consumed, for his compassions never fail.

LAMENTATIONS 3:22

pray & reflect

"The Lord your God is with you; the mighty One will save you. He will rejoice over you. You will rest in his love; he will sing and be joyful about you."
—Zephaniah 3:17 EXB

The Lord your God is with you; the mighty One will save you. He will rejoice over you. You will rest in his love; he will sing & be joyful about you.

ZEPHANIAH 3:17

pray & reflect

"There is no fear in love; instead,
perfect love drives out fear."
—1 John 4:18 HCSB

There is no fear in love; instead, perfect love drives out fear.

1 JOHN 4:18

pray & reflect

"For the mountains may move and the hills disappear,
but even then my faithful love for you will remain."
—Isaiah 54:10 NLT

For the mountains may move and the hills disappear, but even then my faithful love for you will remain.

ISAIAH 54:10

pray & reflect

"May you be able to feel and understand, as all God's children should, how long, how wide, how deep, and how high his love really is."
—Ephesians 3:18 TLB

May you be able to feel & understand, as all God's children should, how long, how wide, how deep, and how high his love really is.

EPHESIANS 3:18

pray & reflect

"O Lord, you are so good, so ready to forgive,
so full of unfailing love for all who ask for your help."
—Psalm 86:5 NLT

O Lord,
you are so good,
so ready to forgive,
so full of unfailing love
for all who ask
for your help.

PSALM 86:5

pray & reflect

"Give thanks to God—
he is good and his love never quits."
—1 Chronicles 16:34 Message

Give thanks
to God,
he is good
&
his love
never quits.

1 CHRONICLES 16:34

pray & reflect

"I give you a new commandment,
that you love one another."
—John 13:34 NRSV

I give you a new commandment, that you love one another.

JOHN 13:34

pray & reflect

"And above all these put on love,
which binds everything together in perfect harmony."
—Colossians 3:14 ESV

And above all
these put on
love, which binds
everything together
in perfect harmony.

COLOSSIANS 3:14

pray & reflect

"Love is patient, love is kind *and* is not jealous;
love does not brag *and* is not arrogant."
—1 Corinthians 13:4 NASB

Love is patient,
love is kind
& is not jealous;
love does not brag
& is not arrogant.

1 CORINTHIANS 13:4

pray & reflect

"There is no greater love
than to lay down one's life for one's friends."
—John 15:13 NLT

There is
no greater love
than to lay down
one's life for
one's friends.

JOHN 15:13

pray & reflect

"Love bears all things, believes all things,
hopes all things, endures all things."
—1 Corinthians 13:7 ESV

Love
bears all
believes
hopes Things
endures

1 CORINTHIANS 13:7

pray & reflect

"Love must be sincere.
Hate what is evil; cling to what is good."
—Romans 12:9 NIV

Love must be sincere.
Hate what is evil;
cling to what is good.

ROMANS 12:9

pray & reflect

"In all things God works for the good of those who love him,
who have been called according to his purpose."
—Romans 8:28 NIV

In all things
God works for the good
of those who love him,
who have been called
according to his purpose.

ROMANS 8:28

pray & reflect

"Do everything in love."
—1 Corinthians 16:14 NIV

Do everything in love.

1 CORINTHIANS 16:14

More Coloring Books From Margaret Feinberg

To learn more about Margaret, visit margaretfeinberg.com.

Drink deeply from Scripture as you relax and meditate on the freedom that comes with knowing who you are in Christ. While you color the intricate designs, connect with the God who unburdens you to be all you were meant to be—and live free.

Live Free

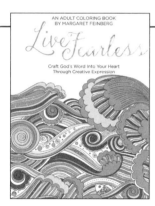

Drink deeply from Scripture while you de-stress and meditate on the courage that comes with knowing God is by your side. God wants us to live bold lives, free of fear. As you color these intricate designs, you'll find the peace and reassurance you need to do so.

Live Fearless

❖ BethanyHouse

 Stay up-to-date on your favorite books and authors with our free e-newsletters. Sign up today at bethanyhouse.com.

Find us on Facebook. facebook.com/BHPnonfiction

Follow us on Twitter. @bethany_house